THEN & NOW

OGUNQUIT

This is a map of Ogunquit drawn by Richard Coolidge, the owner of the Dan Sing Fan, and published in 1927.

THEN & NOW

OGUNQUIT

Kathryn M. Severson,
Susan Day Meffert,
and Marie D. Natoli

Dear Cathe,
You will enjoy these
all the more after you
see Ogunquit this
Cathe, sweetheart
Enjoy the photos Love,
Kathy

*This work is dedicated to Jonathan Alexander Natoli
and his enjoyment of Maine, the way life should be.*
—*Marie D. Natoli*
—*Kathryn M. Severson*

*The book is dedicated also to the memory of Ogunquit's
first families, whose foresightedness and generosity allowed
the natural beauty of Ogunquit to be preserved forever.*
—*Susan Day Meffert*

Copyright © 2009 by Kathryn M. Severson, Susan Day Meffert, and Marie D. Natoli
ISBN 978-0-7385-6535-4

Library of Congress Control Number: 2008940912

Published by Arcadia Publishing
Charleston SC, Chicago IL, Portsmouth NH, San Francisco CA

Printed in the United States of America

For all general information contact Arcadia Publishing at:
Telephone 843-853-2070
Fax 843-853-0044
E-mail sales@arcadiapublishing.com
For customer service and orders:
Toll-Free 1-888-313-2665

Visit us on the Internet at www.arcadiapublishing.com

On the front cover: The historic view of Perkins Cove, taken from the Woodbury studio, shows the original fishing shacks. In the foreground is Eben Ramsdell's fish shack where he dried and sold his catch. Like many of the properties in and around the cove, the fish shack is now a private residence. The modern photograph was also taken from the Woodbury studio, which is owned by Marcia Beal Brazer. (Historic image, courtesy of Katie Rowe; contemporary photograph by Kathryn Severson.)

On the back cover: Shown in this very early photograph of the intersection of Shore Road and Israel's Head Road, the house in the center was built around 1835 by Edward Jacobs. Beyond it is the Baptist church. When this photograph was taken in the 1890s, the house on the left was occupied by Joseph and Lillis Hutchins and was owned for many years by the Keene family. The Ogunquit Memorial Library and its row of high windows are just visible behind the house, and the Colonial and Sachem Hotels stand behind the church on the right. (Courtesy of the Ogunquit Heritage Museum.)

CONTENTS

ACKNOWLEDGMENTS

This book could not have been written without the tremendous help and support of the Ogunquit Heritage Museum (OHM) and its assistant curator Paula Cummings, who spent untold hours searching through the OHM's archives for images from the past and entertained us with her stories at the same time. The museum is housed in the Capt. James Winn house, a building dating from 1780, which became town property when it was moved to the Dorothea Jacobs Grant Common in the center of Ogunquit. The common was given to the town by Grant, a descendant of the founding family of the Sparhawk Hotel.

The Historical Society of Wells and Ogunquit (HSWO) and its administrator Jane Edgecomb were another source of old photographs without which there would be no book. Many of the artifacts of Ogunquit's history are housed at the Historical Society of Wells and Ogunquit because the two towns were a single entity until 1980 when Ogunquit was incorporated as a separate village.

Thanks go to Paula Cummings; Barbara Woodbury, the curator of the Ogunquit Heritage Museum; and to Jane Edgecomb, and thank you to the board of directors of the Historical Society of Wells and Ogunquit who kindly loaned us photographs without charge.

Private citizens who helped us to identify and find historical photographs provided a wealth of information. Thanks to Katie and Harold Rowe, Barbara Grover, John A. and Katherine Goodwin and their daughter Jeanne de Metracopoulos, Alison Seaman Zurlo, Meredith Baker, Carole Lee Carroll, Marcia Brazer, Barry Kean, Louesa Gillespie, Newell Perkins, and Peter Woodbury.

Books from which we drew inspiration and factual information include Charles Littlefield Seaman's *A Pictorial History of Ogunquit, Maine* (1993); *The Cove*, by Carrie Boyd, Kathryn Ryan, Betty Wills, and William Wills (1976); *Ogunquit, Maine, 1900–1971 In Pictures and Words*, by Charles Littlefield Seaman (2001); *Ogunquit By-the-Sea*, John D. Bardwell (1994); *300th Anniversary, Wells, Maine, 1653–1953*, by Esselyn Perkins; and *A Century of Color, 1886–1986* by Louise Tragard, Patricia E. Hart and W. L. Copithorne (1987).

Unless otherwise indicated, all contemporary images were photographed by author Kathryn M. Severson.

Introduction

What a spot. Ogunquit is a town that has for more than two centuries provided something for everyone. Blessed with a saltwater river running to the ocean, a three-mile white sand beach stretching all the way to the next town north, and a cluster of sheltered coves resting at the base of a freshwater river, it was first a fishing ground for Native American tribes in the area and, later, a safe harbor for its dory fishermen. Perkins Cove was called simply the cove or the fish cove by the old dory fishermen. It was named inadvertently by Mrs. Daniel Perkins in the late 1800s, when to differentiate her boardinghouse, the Cove House, from Lyman Staples's Cove House, she called her place the Perkins Cove House, thus naming Perkins Cove forever more. The cove in those days consisted of fish shacks and one house on Adams Island, built by George Adams in 1850. The house was accessible only by boat or by crossing at low tide. It was Adams who started the Cove Fish Company in 1856, consisting of 15 members who drew shares of $25 each for 27 lots in the narrow strip of land leading to Adams Island.

At the other end of town, the late 1800s saw the mouth of the Ogunquit River become a thriving port for seagoing vessels. Sea captains lived in handsome New England cottages in town and plied their trade along the East Coast and beyond, carrying cargo of cordwood to Boston and salt and sand to ports down the coast. Ogunquit's sea captains included Barak Maxwell, Daniel Maxwell, Charles Perkins, and William Hamilton, among others. Their legacy lives on today in the splendid mansions they built.

By the end of the 1800s, the advent of the railroad brought Ogunquit's seagoing commerce to a close, but it also opened up the town to vacationers and that led to the flourishing of Ogunquit's grand hotels, including the Sparhawk, the St. Aspinquid, the Ontio, the Lookout, the Colonial, the Sachem, and the Beachmere. These magnificent properties brought summer visitors in droves and gave Ogunquit a reputation as a gentle, timeless safe haven for families from the cities. Today those families' great-grandchildren are the ones who come back year after year and often retire here.

Blessed with a rocky coastline and its sleepy little fishing cove, Ogunquit attracted artists from earliest times. In 1888, Charles Woodbury, a young Boston art teacher, became acquainted with the area. He is credited with spreading word of the beauties of Ogunquit, and many other artists followed him here. Woodbury built the first art studio, and there he opened his famous art school. He is reputed to have bought five acres of land from Jedediah Moses Perkins for $400 and to have later received the same amount for a painting of the scene.

Barely 20 years later, Hamilton Easter Field, an artist and art critic from New York, arrived, accompanied by his young French protégé, Robert Laurent, to bring the study of modern art and sculpture to Ogunquit's burgeoning art colony. In 1910, Field purchased the Adams house and many of the fish shacks that made up Perkins Cove at the time. He then built a school, the Summer School of Graphic Arts, which produced many famous and talented artists in the 10 years it ran. Closed in 1922 due to the untimely death of Field, it was reopened by Laurent in 1935 and continued developing American talent until 1962.

Ogunquit has never been without benefactors. In 1895, Charles Hoyt built the Victorian estate that became the Beachmere Inn, and his brother Edward Hoyt's wife built the Village Studio and gave Ogunquit its early theatricals. The George M. Connarroe family of Philadelphia built the Ogunquit Memorial Library and St. Peters By the Sea, Nememiah Jacobs built the Sparhawk Hotel, and Samuel Jackson Perkins built the St. Aspinquid Hotel. Israel Littlefield had his Ontio guesthouse, and Walter and Maude Hartwig came to the area in 1930 and built the Ogunquit Playhouse and its resident company of stage luminaries. They then built the new playhouse that ran for almost 50 years under the leadership of John Lane, another benefactor. The art schools brought artists of every stripe, which led to the development of the Ogunquit Art Association, and later the Barn Gallery. Henry Strater, a prominent artist and art collector, built the Ogunquit Museum of American Art, another wonderful gift to the town.

Of course, Ogunquit's most precious gifts are its natural beauties, but they too could have been lost or compromised if it had not been for some other wise benefactors, including Josiah Chase, a Maine legislator, who brought about the preservation of the Marginal Way, and the townspeople, who raised awareness and taxes to preserve the most beautiful white sand beach in Maine from private development. Every step of the way, generous merchants and business owners helped to guard the unique treasures of this town. Many of the town's finest residences spring from and carry the timeless elegance of the former grand hotels and guesthouses. Today visitors can wander down Shore Road, up Main Street, out onto the Marginal Way, and into Perkins Cove and still feel the magic and see the rich history of the place all around them. It is indeed, as the Native Americans knew, a beautiful place by the sea.

Susan Meffert
Marie Natoli
January 2009

CHAPTER 1

PERKINS COVE

This aerial view of Perkins Cove as it appeared before the dredging of 1941 shows footbridge number three. In the extreme left background, the sloping roof of the Dan Sing Fan is barely visible. At the mouth of the cove, the building on the left was built by Hamilton Easter Field as a garage and was at the time of this photograph the Brush and Needle Shop. It later became Barnacle Billy's restaurant. The Island House in the middle foreground was enlarged by Field in 1910 but was still the only building on Adams Island. (Courtesy of Katie Rowe.)

The George Adams house, built in 1850, sat on Adams Island, which was accessible only by boat or by crossing at low tide. Hamilton Easter Field purchased the island, the Adams house, and numerous fishing shacks in the cove in 1902 and created his famous art and sculpture school. Today the same view taken from the bridge shows Field's Island House and many more roofs on the island behind it. (Historic image, courtesy of Carole Lee Carroll.)

Judging by the structure of the bridge, this photograph was probably taken in the early 1900s. The building in the near middle ground was originally Oliver Littlefield's barn, constructed in the 1800s. Today the same view shows a vastly more populated cove. The Littlefield barn, to the left of the raised bridge, is still there. (Historic image, courtesy of OHM.)

The Art Colony, Perkins Cove   Ogunquit, Maine

Moses Lyman Staples constructed the old footbridge around 1900 for the convenience of his guests. This postcard mistook the two buildings in the background for the art center. They were in fact the old icehouse and the building that currently houses the Lobster Shack. These days, the footbridge is raised in winter to accommodate fishing boats coming and going. (Historic image, courtesy of Carole Lee Carroll.)

In the very early photograph below of the Adams house, it sits alone on the island with the channel of water behind it. This is where the ocean ran into the cove in the old days. Today Adams Island is covered with houses, and the old channel into the cove has been filled in. (Historic image, courtesy of Katie Rowe.)

This early 1900s view of the cove depicts the art center (right), built by Hamilton Easter Field in 1910 to house his art school. At left are the Brush and Needle Shop and the Littlefield barn, which became an art studio. The former Brush and Needle Shop is now Barnacle Billy's restaurant, and the Littlefield barn/art studio today houses the Christmas Dove. Now numerous gift shops are housed in the former art school. (Historic image, courtesy of Katie Rowe.)

The ocean side of the cove is called Oarweed Cove. In the right background is Oliver Littlefield's barn, built before 1870, which later became the studio for artist John Hawkins. Today restaurants and shops face the ocean side of the cove. (Historic image, courtesy of OHM.)

A narrow causeway led to the fishing shacks. The art school is in the center, and the bridge that is slightly visible on the far right is the second footbridge built in the cove during the 1920s. (Historic image, courtesy of OHM.)

In the 1930s photograph below, the art center is at left. The tall building on the right is the icehouse, built by Hamilton Easter Field originally to house ice for the fishermen to store their catch. The building was rented in the summer during the 1940s and 1950s and was the scene of many parties and artists' balls. Today the same buildings house gift shops and art galleries. (Historic image, courtesy of HSWO.)

The second footbridge was built in the cove during the 1920s. To its right in the background are Hamilton Easter Field's art center and the old icehouse. This second bridge was constructed prior to the dredging of the canal into the cove. (Historic image, courtesy of OHM.)

In this very early photograph that views Perkins Cove from the north, Eden Ramsdell's fish shack sits in the foreground. In the background, from left to right, are the art center, the icehouse, and the shack (just visible over Ramsdell's in the foreground). The land ends at right. The ocean originally came through that channel, leaving Adams Island inaccessible except at low tide. (Historic image, courtesy of OHM.)

Sometime between 1910 when Hamilton Easter Field enlarged the Island House and 1940 when the footbridge in the cove was rebuilt, this scene shows the edge of the Brush and Needle Shop on the left. The photograph was taken before the dredging of the cove in 1941. The cove today does not differ greatly from the old days except in the number of new buildings. (Historic image, courtesy of OHM.)

A mid-1930s postcard depicts fishermen of the era. From left to right are Herm Knight, Albert Perkins, Warren Hutchins, Leonard Perkins, and Henry Card. The bridge behind them is the second footbridge into the cove. In recent years, there has been a lot of construction in the cove to protect visitors and the infrastructure of the cove itself. (Historic image, courtesy of Susan Meffert.)

Charles Woodbury, the artist who first discovered Ogunquit, built the studio shown at left in the postcard image below from 1896. He opened his famous art school there in 1898 and built his family house behind the studio (second from left). Eben Ramsdell's shack is seen in the middle, and on the right is the annex to the Riverside Hotel. The three buildings in the foreground are still standing and are privately owned. (Historic image, courtesy of Marcia Beal Brazer.)

Beach at Perkins Cove, Ogunquit, Me.

This photograph shows the Island House as it appeared after it was enlarged by Hamilton Easter Field in 1910. It is clear that the ocean flows into the cove from the left in front of the Island House. Now Adams Island is covered with new homes, and the Island House has been remodeled several times. (Historic image, courtesy of HSWO.)

This is the building that housed Hamilton Easter Field's school of art and sculpture. The photograph probably dates to the early 1930s when the school was closed due to the untimely death of Field. It was opened again in 1935 by Field's protégé, Robert Laurent, and ran until 1962. (Historic image, courtesy of HSWO.)

Believed to be the oldest house in Ogunquit, possibly built in 1707 by John Littlefield, it was moved in 1922 from Frazier's Pasture to the cove. According to Charles Seaman's book *A Pictorial History of Ogunquit, Maine 1870–1950*, in the cove, it was first an artists' studio, and in the early 1900s, it became a teahouse known as the Whistling Oyster. Now it is Barnacle Billy's Etc. (Historic image, courtesy of Allison Seaman Zurlo and Meredith Baker.)

After 1922, the studio shown on page 27 became part of the Whistling Oyster, a very popular teahouse. During the years that Ogunquit was a dry town, teahouses flourished, and the Whistling Oyster and the Dan Sing Fan were two of the most popular. The building burned in the 1970s and was rebuilt. Today it houses Barnacle Billy's Etc. restaurant. (Historic image, courtesy of HSWO.)

Seen in this 1938 photograph, the Hubbard house, located on Oarweed Lane, was the second-oldest house in Ogunquit. It is now a converted condominium. (Historic image, courtesy of HSWO.)

The home of early Littlefield family members, this structure was built in the late 1770s by John Littlefield and was the home of Benjamin Littlefield in 1799. Still standing but with a 1928 addition, it is now a popular gift shop. (Historic image, courtesy of HSWO.)

The Dan Sing Fan was a famous teahouse built in 1920. This view shows how it looked from the water's edge at the back of Perkins Cove. The building was torn down by the town in the mid–1980s, and in its place, three residences were constructed. (Historic image, courtesy of Barry Kean.)

Dàn Sing Fan Tea and Gift Shop, Ogunquit, Maine   Hand Colored

The photograph below shows how the porch of the Dan Sing Fan looked during the 1920s and 1930s. The teahouse, overlooking the cove, was famous for its cinnamon toast made with powdered sugar and its jasmine tea. The tearoom was first opened by invitation only on Tuesday, June 28, 1921. Sixty summer guests and residents gathered for sandwiches, cake, Chinese fruit punch, and tea served by Richard Coolidge and Luigi Balestro, according to a 2008 article in the *York County Coast Star* by Sharon Cummins. Today this hillside overlooking the cove is covered by three private residences, of which this is one. (Historic image, courtesy of Barry Kean.)

Tea Porch, Dan Sing Fan, Ogunquit, Maine   Hand Colored

The Riverside Hotel began as a boardinghouse owned by Lyman Staples in the late 1800s. Although there has been considerable change to its buildings, the resort has remained in the Staples family ever since. (Historic image, courtesy of OHM.)

The Ramsdell house, dating from 1909, sits at the corner of Pine Hill South and Shore Road. Eben Ramsdell dried fish on the ledges behind the house. It has been in the Goodwin family for 40 years and looks today very much like it looked in 1909. (Historic image, courtesy of John A. Goodwin.)

Ramsdell is standing on Pine Hill South in 1922. According to Kevin O'Neil, the house, owned by the O'Neils from the 1940s to the 1980s, was later turned into a bed and breakfast. It appears almost unchanged today. (Historic image, courtesy of John A. and Catherine Goodwin.)

The Hillcrest Hotel overlooks Perkins Cove and stands at the corner of Shore Road and Pine Hill South in this photograph from about 1950. It was the only hotel in Ogunquit (because it was south of the York town line) that could serve liquor until the late 1960s when Ogunquit went wet. Today the Hillcrest consists of condominiums and time-share apartments. (Historic image, courtesy of the HSWO.)

In 1937, the view of Perkins Cove and the Ramsdell house from the porch at the Hillcrest Hotel was magnificent. Today the trees prevent this kind of panoramic view. (Historic image, courtesy of John A. and Katherine Goodwin.)

This is one of the earliest photographs of Pine Hill, taken from the intersection of Pine Hill North and Shore Road probably in 1915. The hill itself is completely obscured today by trees, but it is in the process of being developed into new residences. (Historic image, courtesy of Barry Kean.)

Here is an 1890s photograph of the barn and chicken coop that sat at the corner of Pine Hill North and Shore Road. The buildings were converted into living space and the Mountford Coolidge Antique Shop in the early 1900s. The buildings have gone through numerous transformations, first as shops and later as a bed and breakfast and private residences. (Historic image, courtesy of Barry Kean.)

Built by Amos Littlefield in the early 1800s, this building stands at the foot of Pine Hill North. During the late 1800s, it served as a trolley stop and was the Walnut Grove boarding house. Extensively remodeled during the 1940s, it became a weaver's studio. Later it was a restaurant known as Poor Richard's Tavern, owned and operated by Richard Perkins until the late 1990s. It is now a condominium. (Historic image, courtesy of Carole Lee Carroll.)

This is the Staples farm on Shore Road in the early 1900s. Frank Keyes had an ice business here, and it was also run as a guesthouse called Unity Inn. Today it is a private residence called Cocklebutton Farm. (Historic image, courtesy of OHM.)

St. Peter's by the Sea Episcopal Church, located on Shore Road just south of the Cliff House, has been standing since 1897 and opens up to local and visiting congregations each summer. It was built by George M. Connarroe of Philadelphia, whose wife built the Ogunquit Memorial Library in his memory. The masonry is said to have been done by Jedidiah Perkins. The only thing that has changed is the size of the trees that surround it. (Historic image, courtesy of OHM.)

THE VILLAGE

This is an aerial view of Ogunquit Village, which must have been taken after 1930 when Walter and Maude Hartwig bought the first Ogunquit Playhouse and added the tall part of the building as the stage area (seen at approximately two o'clock). The St. Aspinquid is visible at the base of Beach Street on the left. (Historic image, courtesy of Katie Rowe.)

Seen in this postcard mailed in 1933, the Chapman house, located at Shore Road and Bourne Lane, served as a boardinghouse in the early days of the Ogunquit Playhouse and later became part of the Pink Blossom Resort. (Historic image, courtesy of Carole Lee Carroll.)

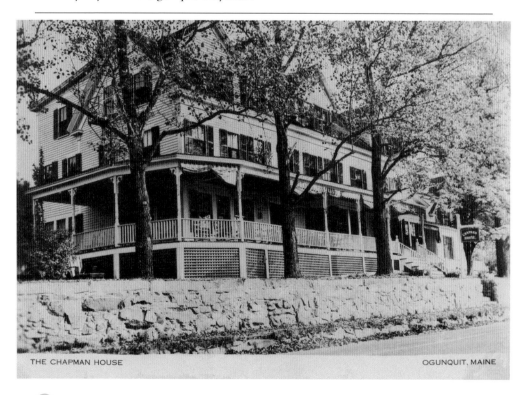

THE CHAPMAN HOUSE   OGUNQUIT, MAINE

This is a 1910 photograph of the library and the Baptist church (after it was raised to two stories). The porch in the left foreground belongs to the Keene house. Behind the church are the Colonial Hotel (left) and the Sachem Hotel (right). The same view today is obscured by trees, but the library and the church remain exactly the same. (Historic image, courtesy of Katie Rowe.)

The earliest building of the Lookout Hotel was constructed in 1883. It was a rooming house owned by Israel Littlefield that was sold to the Merrill family in 1897. The building was expanded in the early 1930s by Malcolm and Oliver Merrill. The lovely giant that was the Lookout became the first condominium conversion in Ogunquit when it was sold in 1977. Today the complex offers its owners extraordinary views of the town, the Marginal Way, and the ocean. (Historic image, courtesy of Katie Rowe.)

The Ontio Hotel, sitting atop Ontio Hill next door to the Lookout Hotel, was actually the first grand hotel on the hill, built in the 1880s by partners Oliver Merrill and Hobbs Knight. The hotel burned on September 30, 1934, and was rebuilt. It remained one of Ogunquit's grand hotels until 1984. Today it houses condominiums with spectacular views overlooking the Ogunquit River, the beach, and the ocean. (Historic image, courtesy of OHM.)

This is the Sachem Hotel, located between the Baptist church and the Colonial Hotel on Shore Road, as it looked in the 1930s. The hotel was torn down sometime in the 1970s to make room for a church parking lot. The church (right) and the Colonial Hotel are still in existence today. (Historic image, courtesy of OHM.)

Colonial Inn, Ogunquit, Maine.

In 1921, the Colonial Hotel was one of the many grand-style hotels in Ogunquit on Shore Road north of the Baptist church. It is still operating as a hotel with a more modern configuration. (Historic image, courtesy of Carole Lee Carroll.)

The Beachmere Ogunquit, Maine

Here is the Beachmere Inn as it looked in 1937 following its purchase by Malcolm and Anne Merrill from Charles Hoyt. It was bought in 1936 and opened in 1937. It became one of the most recognized of Ogunquit's hotels because of its early cottage-style architecture. Although there have been numerous additions, the basic cottage is still visible today. (Historic image, courtesy of Carole Lee Carroll.)

This photograph may have been taken before 1936 when the Beachmere Inn was still part of the Hoyt estate. It was taken from the direction of Shore Road. Although greatly expanded, the original building is still visible in the center of the resort today. (Historic image, courtesy of OHM.)

The Barbara Dean Restaurant, shown below in one of its earliest views, was originally the home of William Henry Perkins. Later it was run as the famous Barbara Dean Restaurant first by Virginia Knapp and her mother and then by the Ireland family. Now it has been transformed into condominiums. The original building still stands at the Shore Road entrance to the Marginal Way. (Historic image, courtesy of HSWO.)

The Post House, one of the oldest commercial buildings in Ogunquit at the corner of Shore Road and School Street, was used as a dance hall, a store, and a post office. In later years, it was an annex to Sparhawk Hall. It is currently a guesthouse called the Parsons Post House Inn. (Historic image, courtesy of HSWO.)

Built prior to 1872 and owned by Samuel Littlefield Jr., this was an early restaurant that later became Bernard's Bakery. Today a greatly expanded building houses the Blueberry Café at the corner of Cottage Street and Shore Road. (Historic image, courtesy of Allison Seaman Zurlo and Meredith Baker.)

The Sparhawk Hotel, then called Spearhawk Hall, was built in 1897 by Nememiah Jacobs and burned to the ground on October 4, 1899. It was completely rebuilt. The Sparhawk Oceanfront Resort continues in the tradition of Ogunquit's grandest and oldest hotels. (Historic image, courtesy of HSWO.)

Seen below, this view of Sparhawk Hall was photographed in 1928 from Shore Road. It was rebuilt by its owner, Nememiah Jacobs, in 1899. The grand hotel was one of the most recognizable institutions in Ogunquit until late in the 1900s. It could accommodate 250 guests. (Historic image, courtesy of John A. Goodwin.)

The Jacobs family poses in front of the Jacobs homestead, which was built on Shore Road during the 1880s. The building is considerably changed but stands today as part of the modern Sparhawk Oceanfront Resort. (Historic image, courtesy of HSWO.)

At the corner of Shore Road and Israel's Head Road, a 1920s trolley rounds the bend in front of Gus Keene's house. The Keene house was home to many of the playhouse actors, stagehands, and colony students from the 1930s until the mid-1960s. In recent times, the smaller house to the left has been both a store and a restaurant known as Amore Breakfast. (Historic image, courtesy of Katie Rowe.)

In the early days of Sparhawk Hall, there were riding stables in the field across Shore Road from the hotel. In this 1948 photograph of the still-existent stables, guests prepare for a morning's ride. The field where these stables stood is now the Dorothea Jacobs Grant Common, which was given to the town in the 1990s and developed around the Ogunquit Heritage Museum at the Capt. James Winn house. The common sits behind the Obed's Lane parking lot. (Historic image, courtesy of Paula Cummings.)

The photograph below, taken around 1930, shows the original Winn family house, located at that time on Route 1 north. The original building dates from 1780 and is one of the oldest in Ogunquit. The house was given to the town by a Perkins descendant and then moved. Some years later, an ad hoc committee of concerned citizens moved it again in order to preserve it and to establish the Ogunquit Heritage Museum in it. (Historic image, courtesy of HSWO.)

THE VILLAGE

The origins of Ogunquit's current Barn Gallery are in the Ogunquit Art Association housed in the barn attached to the Sea Chambers hotel. In this 1950s photograph, it is still in that location on Shore Road across from Cottage Street. Today the building is part of the Sea Chambers resort. (Historic image, courtesy of HSWO.)

In the late 19th century, Wharf Lane was the access route to many of the fish houses that were clustered along the banks of the Ogunquit River. Little changed today, the entrance to Wharf Lane is now part of the Marginal Way, and the same buildings house the Ogunquit Camera Shop on the left and a clothing shop on the right. (Historic image, courtesy of John A. Goodwin.)

In 1939, Walter and Maude Hartwig built a 700-seat theater on Route 1 south of the village. The new Ogunquit Playhouse was bought by John and Helen Lane in 1951, and in the heyday of the straw-hat circuit, it was one of the premiere summer theaters in the country. It continues to be one of Ogunquit's greatest treasures 76 years later. (Historic image, courtesy of Carole Lee Carroll.)

THE OGUNQUIT PLAYHOUSE—FAMOUS FROM NOVA SCOTIA TO SAN DIEGO FOR ITS STARS AND PRODUCTIONS, WITH REAL ACTORS ON A REGULAR STAGE

The Ogunquit Village School, located on School Street, was opened in 1906. The building was condemned in 2005, and the school closed in 2006 for lack of pupils. Today the building and the surrounding playground make up a part of the town management property. The building is currently empty. (Historic image, courtesy of HSWO.)

This early photograph offers a view of Ogunquit village at the mouth of Shore Road and was taken before 1927 when the trolley stopped running. On the left, just visible with two dormers, is Dr. J. W. Gordon's house. To its right is the Perkins Block, built in 1907. The Perkins Block now houses the Front Porch and other shops. (Historic image, courtesy of Katie Rowe.)

An early 1930s photograph of Shore Road looking north from School Street on the left and the Methodist church on the right shows a number of fine old capes and colonial houses. These homes now provide settings for numerous art galleries, gift shops, specialty stores, and restaurants. (Historic image, courtesy of Marie Natoli.)

At the corner of Shore Road and Beach Street, Dr. J. W. Gordon's home and office stood for many years. The Perkins Block, built in 1907, stood next to it. In the early 1950s, the town bought the property at auction and razed the building to widen the mouth of Beach Street. Today a veterans' park has been established in its place, and the Front Porch, a popular restaurant, operates in what was originally the Perkins Block. (Historic image, courtesy of HSWO.)

The photograph below of Beach Street (then called Ocean Avenue) was taken from the High Rock Hotel in the 1930s. The building that today houses Abacus is in the right foreground, and just behind it is Dr. J. W. Gordon's house on the corner of Shore Road and Beach Street. In the modern image, the building with a tall rear portion was first the Ogunquit Playhouse in 1933 and later the Ogunquit Square movie theater. The building contains restaurants, shops, and a private residence today. (Historic image, courtesy of Katie Rowe.)

Bird's-Eye View of Ocean Avenue, Ogunquit, Me.

A 1908 photograph of Ogunquit Square is looking south to the entrance of Shore Road. The building in the left foreground was Joe Littlefield's store and post office. The building was moved in the early 1920s, and the site was a Gulf service station for many years. It is now an outdoor seating area for the Village Food Market. The building at right, partly blocked by the electric trolley, is known as Bessie's Restaurant today. (Historic image, courtesy of Katie Rowe.)

The Maxwell House, one of Ogunquit's earliest boardinghouses, provided a summer residence for many of the apprentices, actors, and stagehands from the playhouse each year from the 1930s until the 1960s. Originally it was a boardinghouse called the Rockland. It was razed in 1972, and a branch of Key Bank was built in its place. (Historic image, courtesy of Katie Rowe.)

In the years before the automobile, the original C. L. Maxwell store, located at the corner of Berwick Road and Main Street, sold cold drinks, fruit, cigars, and tobacco according to the sign. Maxwell's operated as a grocery and hardware store for almost 70 years. Now the building is the home of Maxwell's Pub. (Historic image, courtesy of HSWO.)

This early photograph shows a homestead in the village north of the town center that may have belonged to Barak Maxwell. Today the building, little changed on the outside, houses the Scotch Hill Inn. (Historic image, courtesy of OHM.)

Another early homestead, located on Route 1 heading north out of Ogunquit, is now known as the Black Boar Inn. (Historic image, courtesy of OHM.)

In 1913, Merry Delle Hoyt, a summer resident from St. Louis, designed and built the Village Studio where for 15 years she staged amateur theatricals and pageants that became well known to Ogunquit's summer visitors and residents alike. Today the building on Hoyts Lane is a private residence. (Historic image, courtesy of HSWO.)

The Ogunquit Lobster Pound on Route 1 opened in 1936. Run by the Hancock family since the 1930s, it has become a landmark for generations of vacationing families. (Historic image, courtesy of OHM.)

At the head of Beach Street on the left-hand side, the Betty Doon Restaurant and Motel, pictured here in 1936, has been a fixture in Ogunquit for many years. Known today as the Betty Doon Motor Hotel, the building has been expanded, and since the 1960s, it has also housed numerous shops. (Historic image, courtesy of OHM.)

Two grand hotels, Sparhawk Hall and the St. Aspinquid, opened in Ogunquit in 1897. The St. Aspinquid, at the foot of Beach Street, was built by Samuel Jackson Perkins. The historic photograph shows the hotel after the first expansion. In the 1970s, the property was sold to the Andrews family, and it was torn down and replaced by a motel. The historic image was provided by Pat Pope, a granddaughter of S. J. Perkins.

Across Beach Street from the St. Aspinquid Hotel, Samuel Jackson Perkins built his own house in 1903. Although it has been through many additions and structural changes, the facade appears relatively unchanged today. (Historic image, courtesy of HSWO.)

THE MARGINAL WAY

In this aerial view of the shoreline of Ogunquit, the Marginal Way can be seen as a path along the rocks. The photograph was probably taken before 1940 because the cove had not yet been dredged. It was dredged in 1941. (Courtesy of Katie Rowe).

In 1923, the Marginal Way was given as a gift to the town of Ogunquit by Josiah Chase, a legislator in York. He did this by acquiring easements from land owners in Ogunquit to make it a public path that ran along the cliffs and shoreline for 1.25 miles. It was called the Marginal Way because it was defined originally by the easterly margins of multiple properties. (Historic image, courtesy of OHM.)

Ogunquit's three-mile white sand beach is visible from almost every point on the Marginal Way. The mile-long path leads from Perkins Cove to Shore Road and picks up again at Wharf Lane and runs to the beach. It has been preserved and protected by the town since its earliest days in 1925. In this exact spot along the path, the Marginal Way was dedicated by the town in 1946. (Historic image, courtesy of OHM.)

Coming out of Perkins Cove on the Marginal Way in the early 1900s, one could look back on the cove and see the Hillcrest Hotel far away on the horizon (center left). The barn on the right served as an artist's studio and much later became the Christmas Dove shop. Following severe erosion in recent storms, portions of the Marginal Way have had to be fenced and reinforced on the ocean side. (Historic image, courtesy of OHM.)

The Marginal Way is a treasure that the Town of Ogunquit is working very hard to keep as pristine as possible. It has suffered serious damage in recent years, but the Marginal Way Improvement Association and generous citizens strive continuously to preserve it. In recent years, protection has also been provided to the ecological environment and the vegetation. (Historic image, courtesy of OHM.)

Ontio Beach is one of the small sand-and-rock beaches that lies along the Marginal Way. Although the land adjoining the Marginal Way is now full of houses, little has changed since the early 1900s in the configuration of these small beaches. (Historic image, courtesy of OHM.)

CHAPTER 4

THE RIVER AND THE BEACH

This photograph of the *Ocean Eagle* dates to August 22, 1887. The ship was built in June 1870 by Barak Maxwell. Seen in the background are the wharves from which ships picked up cordwood to be carried to Boston for sale. Also to the left of the vessel stands the Methodist church. (Historic image, courtesy of John A. Goodwin.)

Ogunquit River and Bridge, Ogunquit, Me.

This photograph shows the Ogunquit River after the first bridge was built in 1888 and prior to the construction of the Spearhawk in 1897. Some of the wharves and fish houses are visible in the upper left. By the end of the 1800s, the advent of the railroad brought Ogunquit's seagoing commerce to a close, but it also opened up the town to vacationers. Today the wharves are gone, and the Marginal Way runs down Wharf Lane and across to Beach Street and the bridge. (Historic image, courtesy of OHM.)

The aerial view below, taken after 1888 of Ogunquit Beach and the river, shows the Beachmere at right and the Sparhawk on the riverside to the left. Today one can capture this view of the beach only from high up on Ontio Hill, which makes the Marginal Way all the more welcoming to current visitors. (Historic image, courtesy of OHM.)

In 1888, a bridge was erected over the Ogunquit River, giving access to the beach. Shortly thereafter, the earliest grand hotels of Ogunquit—the Sparhawk and the St. Aspinquid—were built to accommodate summer guests. The largest building in the background has been identified by various townspeople as having been a casino and a dance hall. (Historic image, courtesy of Katie Rowe.)

A photograph from the 1800s shows the Ogunquit River wharves with Ogunquit dories in the foreground and a schooner and the old bridge in the background. (Historic image, courtesy HSWO.)

Here are the fishing shacks in the Ogunquit River in the late 1800s. Note the Sparhawk Hotel in the background. (Historic image, courtesy of Katie Rowe.)

THE RIVER AND THE BEACH

In the early 1900s, dolphin posts still stood as a reminder of the early seagoing days in Ogunquit. The posts stood at the mouth of the river so that schooners could tie up there until the tide was higher. Today the banks of the river have been reinforced against erosion, and the view toward the beach can be seen by pedestrians following the Marginal Way extension from Wharf Lane. (Historic image, courtesy of OHM.)

The photograph below dates from the late 1800s and shows the fish houses, wharves, and the old bridge to the beach. The tallest building at the beach is thought to have housed the first bowling alley in 1906.

In 2008, a new bridge linked the beach to the town, and nothing remained of the early wharves (Historic image, courtesy of HSWO.)

Here is the Perkins Bathing Pavilion at the beach about 1889. The pavilion was owned by Walter Perkins, who lived in the house seen to the right of it. The pavilion burned in March 1941. Today a greatly expanded building houses the Norseman Resort. (Historic image, courtesy of Katie Rowe.)

Sometime around 1923, the village was at risk of losing the beach when an individual acquired a quit claim deed from the state of Maine and began plans to develop it. A group of concerned citizens went to the legislature that year to create the Ogunquit Beach District. The town was allowed to buy the beach for $45,000 in taxes. To save the beach from being developed as private residences, it became a public park. (Historic image, courtesy of HSWO.)

THE RIVER AND THE BEACH

Ogunquit Beach, as seen below in the 1940s, was once famous for its tall and heavily grassed dunes that ran the length of the beach to Wells. During a storm in 1978, the ocean broke through the dunes in some places. The U.S. Army Corps of Engineers replaced sand and reshaped the dunes. (Historic image, courtesy of HSWO.)

ACROSS AMERICA, PEOPLE ARE DISCOVERING SOMETHING WONDERFUL. *THEIR HERITAGE.*

Arcadia Publishing is the leading local history publisher in the United States. With more than 3,000 titles in print and hundreds of new titles released every year, Arcadia has extensive specialized experience chronicling the history of communities and celebrating America's hidden stories, bringing to life the people, places, and events from the past. To discover the history of other communities across the nation, please visit:

www.arcadiapublishing.com

Customized search tools allow you to find regional history books about the town where you grew up, the cities where your friends and family live, the town where your parents met, or even that retirement spot you've been dreaming about.

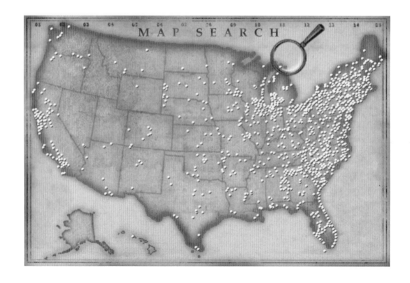